The Bermuda Triangle

ABDO
Publishing Company

The Bermuda Triangle

By Christine Zuchora-Walske

Content Consultant
W. Sean Chamberlin, PhD
Professor, Earth Sciences
Fullerton College

CREDITS

Published by ABDO Publishing Company, PO Box 398166, Minneapolis, MN 55439. Copyright © 2012 by Abdo Consulting Group, Inc. International copyrights reserved in all countries. No part of this book may be reproduced in any form without written permission from the publisher. The Essential Library™ is a trademark and logo of ABDO Publishing Company.

Printed in the United States of America,
North Mankato, Minnesota
102011
012012

 THIS BOOK CONTAINS AT LEAST 10% RECYCLED MATERIALS.

Editor: Melissa York
Copy Editor: Kathryn-Ann Geis
Series design: Becky Daum, Christa Schneider, & Ellen Schofield
Cover and interior production: Christa Schneider

Library of Congress Cataloging-in-Publication Data
Zuchora-Walske, Christine.
  The Bermuda Triangle / by Christine Zuchora-Walske.
      p. cm. -- (Unsolved mysteries)
  Includes bibliographical references.
  ISBN 978-1-61783-298-7
  1. Bermuda Triangle--Juvenile literature. I. Title.
  G558.Z83 2012
  001.94--dc23
                                        2011039152

Table of Contents

Chapter 1

Flight 19

In the early afternoon of December 5, 1945, Lieutenant Charles Taylor pondered the work that lay ahead of him. He was a flight instructor at the Naval Air Station (NAS) in Fort Lauderdale, Florida.

Taylor was scheduled to lead a training group called Flight 19. The group consisted of five Avenger torpedo bombers. Taylor would fly one plane. The rest of the group was comprised of four student pilots and nine student crewmen.

Taylor had just transferred to Fort Lauderdale. He had more than 2,500 hours of flying time under his belt. He was a seasoned pilot and instructor—but he did not feel good

about leading
Flight 19 that day.

Navigation Problem Number One

Flight 19 would
perform an exercise
called Navigation
Problem Number
One. Because
Taylor was a new
instructor at NAS

The Avenger

The Avenger had a reputation for being a tough airplane. The navy had begun using Avengers in 1942, during World War II (1939–1945). "Pilots loved them," said Mark Evans of the Naval Historical Center. "They were built like tanks. Time and again they'd come back from battle all shot up and still functioning."[1]

These airborne tanks were heavy, weighing 10,555 pounds (4,788 kg) when empty. If a pilot had to ditch an Avenger, the plane usually disappeared beneath the waves quickly.

Fort Lauderdale, he had never flown this exercise
before. Neither had his students.

The exercise would test the students' navigation
and bombing skills. They would fly 56 miles (90 km)
east to Hen and Chickens Shoals, a reef lying
between Florida and the Bahamas, where they would
practice bombing. Then they would continue east for
another 67 miles (108 km). Next, the group would
turn north-northwest and fly 73 miles (117 km) to
the northernmost reaches of the Bahamas. Finally,
the planes would turn southwest and fly 120 miles
(193 km) back to Fort Lauderdale.

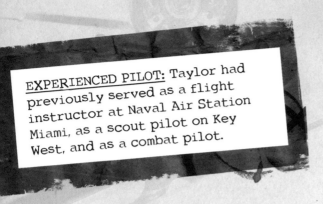

EXPERIENCED PILOT: Taylor had previously served as a flight instructor at Naval Air Station Miami, as a scout pilot on Key West, and as a combat pilot.

Flight 19 was scheduled to take off at 1:45 p.m. Before takeoff, the planes underwent a preflight check. Their fuel tanks contained enough fuel to last more than five hours, until at least 6:45 p.m., and the exercise was scheduled to last approximately three hours, until 4:45 p.m. Survival gear was in good condition, and all instruments were functional. None of the planes had a clock, but this was common. Navy pilots often removed the clocks from their planes and kept them as souvenirs.

The students gathered in the training office, waiting for Taylor to arrive. Taylor showed up at 1:15 p.m. He told his supervisor that he did not want to do the training flight. He asked for a replacement instructor. No replacement was available. So Taylor briefed the students and went over the weather report for the training area. It included scattered rain showers, low clouds, moderate winds, and moderate-to-rough seas. According to navy standards, the weather was good enough for a training flight.

Flight 19 took off at 2:10 p.m. The first leg of the exercise went smoothly.

The Second Leg

Flight 19 should have been finishing the second leg of the exercise around 4:00 p.m. At that time, Robert Cox, a senior flight instructor who happened to be traveling over Fort Lauderdale in his plane, overheard a radio conversation. A voice repeatedly asked a person named Powers what his compass read. Powers was Edward Powers, one of the student pilots in Flight 19. "I don't know where we are," Powers replied. "We must have got lost after that last turn."[2]

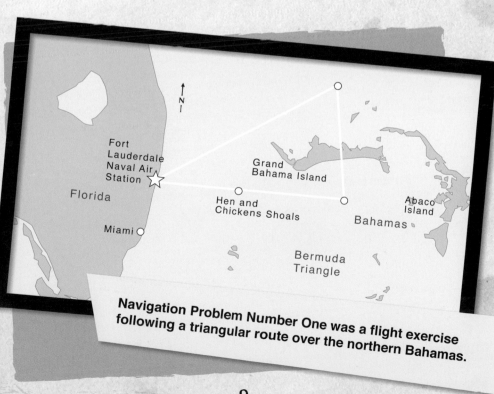

Navigation Problem Number One was a flight exercise following a triangular route over the northern Bahamas.

Cox listened some more and soon identified the first voice as Taylor. Cox radioed Taylor and asked him to explain his trouble. Taylor replied, "Both my compasses are out and I am trying to find Fort Lauderdale, Florida. I am over land but it's broken. I am sure I'm in the Keys but I don't know how far down and I don't know how to get to Fort Lauderdale."[3]

That was an odd thing to say. The Florida Keys are an island chain southwest of mainland Florida, in the Gulf of Mexico. Flight 19 should have been northeast of Fort Lauderdale, over the Atlantic Ocean. But Cox figured that Taylor knew what he

NAS Fort Lauderdale as seen from the air

was talking about. Taylor had spent a lot of time flying over the keys. So Cox told Taylor how to get to Fort Lauderdale from the keys without a compass. Cox also offered to fly south and meet Flight 19 along the way.

Taylor protested. Then he described what had happened earlier: "On the second leg I thought they were going wrong, so I took over and was flying them back to the right position. But I'm sure, now, that neither one of my compasses is working."[4] He also mentioned he had just passed over a small island. No other land was in sight.

Taylor's descriptions troubled Cox. If Taylor were flying toward the mainland along the keys, he would not lose sight of land. Cox insisted on flying to meet Flight 19.

Something Is Wrong

As Cox flew south, Taylor's radio transmissions got weaker. They should have been getting stronger if the two planes were approaching each other.

Cox radioed Taylor: "Your transmissions are fading. Something is wrong."[5] Cox realized that Taylor must be traveling away from him, not toward him. Cox guessed that Flight 19 was not over the keys but over the Atlantic. Since Taylor had lost sight of land, he must be headed northward from the Bahamas.

When Cox was approximately 40 miles (64 km) south of Fort Lauderdale, he lost radio contact with Taylor. Cox turned around and headed home.

Meanwhile, Port Everglades, a rescue unit near Fort Lauderdale, made radio contact with Taylor. At 4:31 p.m., Taylor told Port Everglades that one of his students thought Flight 19 should head west to hit land. Taylor, however, still thought they were in the keys. At 4:45 p.m., he said that he planned to lead the group north-northeast for 45 minutes, "then we will fly north to make sure we are not over the Gulf of Mexico."[6] The squadron had no more than two hours of fuel remaining.

Fly Toward the Sun

When Cox arrived back at Fort Lauderdale, he asked permission to fly over the northern Bahamas to look for Flight 19. Lieutenant Commander Donald Poole denied Cox's request. Poole had a plane prepared to go, but he was reluctant to send it out until Flight 19's position was better known. And Poole had already ordered Port Everglades to tell Taylor he should head west, or "fly toward the sun."[7]

Port Everglades did so. It also asked the various Florida naval air stations to try locating Flight 19 via radar and radio. It asked commercial ships in the area to keep a sharp lookout and alerted the Coast Guard.

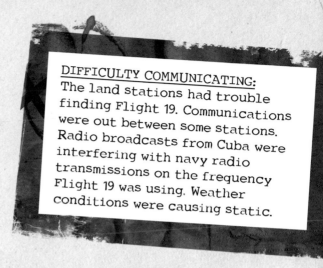

The land stations could often hear transmissions from Flight 19, but many of their transmissions to Flight 19 went unacknowledged. Without a clear, consistent radio connection with Flight 19, it was hard to pinpoint the planes' location. It was hard to help them, too.

At 5:03 p.m., Taylor ordered Flight 19 to fly east for ten minutes. Poole heard two different students reply with frustration. One of them said, "Dammit, if we could just fly west we would get home."[8]

Foul Weather Approaching

At 5:15 p.m., Taylor told Port Everglades that Flight 19 was now flying west. The planes planned to head west until they either reached land or ran out of gas.

Poole was about to order a plane out of Fort Lauderdale to look for Flight 19. But staff informed him that a location would be available soon and that Flight 19 was heading west at last. So at 5:36 p.m.,

Poole decided to hold the plane on the ground. It was getting dark, and foul weather was moving in from the north.

The land stations continued to have difficulty making radio contact with Taylor. At least seven times between 5:00 p.m. and 6:00 p.m., Port Everglades asked Taylor to change his radio from the training frequency he was using to an emergency frequency. The emergency frequency would provide interference-free transmission. It would allow more land stations to communicate with Taylor.

But if Taylor switched, the other four planes would have to switch, too. Taylor feared that Flight 19 might be unable to get together on the frequency. They would then be unable to communicate with one another, and he would lose control of the group. At 5:55 p.m. Taylor said, "I cannot change frequency. I must keep my planes intact."[9]

We All Go Down Together

At 6:00 p.m., the land stations finally calculated Flight 19's location. At 5:50 p.m., Flight 19 had been within 100 miles (160 km) of 29° north latitude and 79° west longitude. That was east of New Smyrna Beach, Florida, and north of the Bahamas.

Avengers in formation. Taylor understood the importance of keeping the planes together.

Fort Lauderdale received this information by phone at 6:10 p.m. All the land stations turned on their airfield lights, beacons, and searchlights to help guide Flight 19 to land.

Meanwhile, radio operators on land heard intermittent, garbled transmissions from Flight 19. Taylor was apparently still struggling with the idea that he was over the Gulf of Mexico. He suggested to his students that they fly due east until they ran out of gas. He said they would have a better chance of rescue closer to shore.

The land stations could not get through to Flight 19, so they could not determine whether it was heading west or east. They kept trying to contact Flight 19, but no one in the group radioed in their location to the listening operators.

LOST AND FOUND: This was not the first time Taylor had gotten lost on the job. It had happened twice during the time he served in World War II. Both times Taylor lost his way, ditched his plane in the ocean, and survived in a life raft until he was rescued.

At approximately 6:20 p.m., the land stations heard an ominous transmission from Flight 19. An unidentified voice said, "All planes close up tight . . . we'll have to ditch unless landfall

. . . when the first plane drops below 10 gallons, we all go down together."[10] Best estimates at this point predicted the squadron could stay airborne for another 20 minutes. After that point, any rescue would be pulling survivors from the ocean.

Flying Boats

At the same time, a rescue plane took off from the Coast Guard Air Station (CGAS) at Dinner Key in Miami. This plane was a Martin Mariner, popularly called a "flying boat"—an airplane that could land on water, float indefinitely, and also take off from the water. It tried to contact Flight 19 from the air, but its radio antenna iced over, knocking out communications.

The weather was worsening. A tanker called the *Viscount Empire* was northeast of the Bahamas and headed for Fort Lauderdale. The tanker told Port Everglades that it was experiencing "tremendous seas and winds of high velocity."[11]

During the next 45 minutes, Port Everglades heard a few garbled transmissions from Flight 19. It seemed that Taylor and student pilot Joseph Bossi were trying to figure out their position and direction. Port Everglades radioed Bossi repeatedly, without success. At 7:04 p.m., Bossi radioed Taylor.

A Martin Mariner, or flying boat

He received no answer. This was the last transmission anyone heard from Flight 19.

Just before 7:30 p.m., two more Mariners took off in search of Flight 19. They left from Banana River NAS, approximately 50 miles (80 km) south of New Smyrna Beach. Each of these crafts carried 13 men. One rescue plane, called *Training 32*, would head directly for Flight 19's last known location. The other plane, called *Training 49*, would fly up the coast to New Smyrna Beach and then due east to the same location. Together, the flying boats would conduct an expanding search of the area.

At 7:30 p.m., *Training 49* confirmed its departure via radio to Banana River. Its next radio report was due at 8:30 p.m.

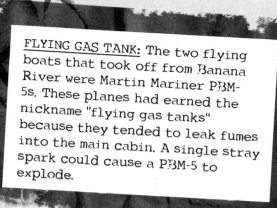

FLYING GAS TANK: The two flying boats that took off from Banana River were Martin Mariner PBM-5s. These planes had earned the nickname "flying gas tanks" because they tended to leak fumes into the main cabin. A single stray spark could cause a PBM-5 to explode.

A Burst of Flames

The 8:30 p.m. report never came. At 8:35 p.m., Banana River tried contacting *Training 49*. Banana River kept trying for an hour with no luck.

At 9:15 p.m., Banana River's commanding officer got a message from a tanker called the *Gaines Mills* cruising approximately 25 miles (40 km) east of New Smyrna Beach: "At [7:50 p.m. we] observed burst of flames, apparently [an] explosion, leaping flames 100 feet (30 m) high burning [for] ten minutes. . . . [At 8:19 p.m. we] stopped [and] circled area using search lights, looking for survivors. None found."[12] The message said the *Gaines Mills* was currently "passing through big pool of oil."[13] Crew members spotted debris but could not pick it up because the sea was too rough.

A US Navy aircraft carrier called the *Solomons* confirmed the *Gaines Mills*'s message. The *Solomons* reported that its radar showed *Training 49* taking off, proceeding on course for 20 minutes, then disappearing at the exact spot the *Gaines Mills* described. The next day, water samples taken in the area contained oil.

Fruitless Search

For the next five days, many military and civilian aircraft and ships searched for the six missing planes. On December 10, the weather became so treacherous that authorities finally called off the search.

The navy went on to conduct a months-long investigation. In 1946, it published a report more than 400 pages long. The report stated that a midair explosion had caused the loss of *Training 49*. It identified pilot error on the part of Taylor as the cause of Flight 19's loss.

Taylor's relatives protested. They did not want the deaths of so many men blamed on Taylor. Their persistence paid off. In October 1947, the navy changed its verdict. It assigned blame to "some unexpected and unforeseen development of weather conditions" instead.[14]

No one has ever found bodies or recovered wreckage from either Flight 19 or *Training 49*.

The lack of physical evidence—plus the navy's vague verdict—has lent the combined incidents an air of mystery. Many people have wondered where the wrecks could possibly be. The planes disappeared nearly 70 years ago. The general locations of their loss are known. So why can no one find them? Other people wonder about Taylor. He was a highly experienced pilot. How had he become so lost and confused? Why did the other pilots follow Taylor's directions when they seemed to know he was wrong? Although the navy closed the case, it remains open in many minds.

Edward Powers's family reviews materials about Flight 19. Decades after the disappearance of Powers and Flight 19, mystery still surrounds the incident.

Chapter 2

A Watery Grave

Many people have wondered whether the swath of ocean east of Florida is especially dangerous. Have travelers there encountered more trouble than those in other parts of the world?

For hundreds of years, no one thought so. People knew the ocean was hazardous, and they accepted the trials of sea travel. But a string of disappearances, culminating with Flight 19, began to arouse public suspicion.

The *Rosalie*

On November 6, 1840, the *Times* newspaper of London, England, reported a strange incident

Many ships have disappeared in the stormy Caribbean sea.

that had happened across the Atlantic. The *Times* had received a letter from its correspondent in the Bahamas. The letter, dated August 27, 1840, said that a small Bahamian craft had recently encountered a big, empty ship at sea:

> *A large French vessel, bound from Hamburgh [Germany] to the Havannah [Cuba] . . . was discovered to be completely abandoned. . . . [H]er sails were set, and she did not appear to have sustained any damage. . . . The only living beings found on board were a cat, some fowls, and several canaries half dead with hunger. . . . She is . . . called the* Rosalie. *Of her crew no intelligence has been received.*[1]

What could have happened? The ship and all of its property were unharmed. All seemed well—except that every human on board was gone. The *Rosalie's* valuable cargo of wine, fruit, and silk was in perfect condition. The captain's papers were all in order. The officers' and passengers' fancy cabins looked as if they had only recently been vacated.

The *Rosalie* was towed to Nassau, Bahamas, where it became an object of curiosity and speculation.

The *Cyclops*

The *Cyclops* was a ship named after a race of one-eyed giants in ancient Greek mythology—and it lived up to its name. It was huge, measuring 542 feet (165 m) long and 65 feet (20 m) wide. Large steel derricks and cranes, used to load and unload bulk cargo such as coal, towered over the ship's deck.

During World War I (1914–1918), the *Cyclops* served in the Naval Overseas Transportation Service under Lieutenant Commander George W. Worley. It fueled the many coal-fired ships of the United States and US allies.

UNSAFE COMMUNICATION: During World War I, some vessels avoided unnecessary radio use so they would not expose their location to enemy ships and submarines.

It also transported other cargo as needed to help the US war effort.

On February 16, 1918, the *Cyclops* departed Rio de Janeiro, Brazil. A crew of 306 men staffed the ship. It carried a load of manganese ore meant for the manufacture of weapons in the United States. The cargo was heavy, but Worley and a shipping foreman

The *Cyclops* had heavy equipment on its deck, making it less stable in rough waters.

had supervised the loading. The cargo exceeded the ship's expected capacity, but they were certain the cargo's weight and cargo distribution were safe. One of the *Cyclops*'s engines was damaged. However, an inspector in Brazil had recommended repairing the engine in the United States. So the ship steamed northward.

On March 3, the *Cyclops* stopped at the Caribbean island of Barbados. It left the next day, bound for Chesapeake Bay. The ship had radio equipment, a new technology at the time. But no one received any radio transmissions from the *Cyclops* after it left Barbados.

The *Cyclops* was due to arrive in the United States on March 13. When it failed to show up on schedule, the navy began looking for it. Because of the lack of radio transmissions, naval officials assumed the *Cyclops* encountered trouble early

Newspaper Reports

Newspapers broke the story of the *Cyclops* on April 15. The *New York Times* reported:

Radio calls to the Cyclops from all possible points have been made and vessels sent to search for her along her probable route and areas in which she might be, with no success. . . . The search for the Cyclops still continues, but the Navy Department feels extremely anxious as to her safety.[2]

in its trip, while it was still near the Caribbean islands.

Military officials kept the story quiet for a month while they tried to find the *Cyclops*. On April 14, the navy notified the crew's families and issued a public statement about the loss of the 306 men.

The navy could not explain the *Cyclops*'s disappearance. The weather had been fine in the area where officials believed the *Cyclops* was traveling. An explosion—

"Damned Dutchman"

Some people believed Worley intentionally betrayed, stole, or destroyed the ship he commanded. Worley was a US citizen with an honorable military record. However, he had been born in Germany. During a war with Germany, and in the absence of any clues, such treachery was easy to believe.

C. Ludlow Livingston, the US consul to Barbados, was one believer. In a telegram to the Department of the Navy, he wrote that the *Cyclops*'s crew hated Worley. "Many called him a 'damned Dutchman,'" said Livingston.[3] (*Dutchman* refers to "Deutschland," the German name for Germany.) He suggested that Worley had stopped in Barbados—despite having enough supplies for the trip to Chesapeake Bay—so the *Cyclops* could obtain enough extra fuel and food to "steam direct to Germany" and turn over his ship and crew to the enemy.[4]

The navy investigated this and other claims of enemy activity until 1922. It found no evidence that the *Cyclops*'s loss was motivated by anything to do with World War I. The German government denied any involvement in the ship's disappearance.

accidental or intentional—might have happened, but no one could find any debris or wreckage. Nor could investigators find evidence of an enemy ship or submarine in the area.

"No well-founded reason can be found to explain the *Cyclops* being overdue," said the navy.[5] But guesses and rumors swirled. The most popular theories involved German spies or submarines. Germany was one of the United States' enemies in World War I.

The navy ended its search for the *Cyclops* in May. Loved ones of the crew mourned their loss, with no clues about how, where, or when the *Cyclops* had met its end.

The *Cotopaxi*

Seven years after the *Cyclops* incident, on November 29, 1925, the cargo ship *Cotopaxi* left Charleston, South Carolina. It carried a load of coal bound for Havana, Cuba. It had a crew of 32 men.

On December 1, radio operators in Florida picked up a transmission from the *Cotopaxi*. The vessel was "listing badly."[6] But its crew did not send out a distress call.

That was the last message anyone heard from the *Cotopaxi*. Coast Guard personnel, radio operators, and lighthouse keepers along the Florida coast searched for the ship throughout December, but their efforts yielded nothing. The crew of 32 men was never seen again.

The *Proteus* and *Nereus*

The *Cotopaxi* would not be the last vessel to vanish in this area. Sixteen years later, another incident occurred.

The *Proteus* at the time of its first voyage, between 1910 and 1915

The *Proteus* and the *Nereus* were large supply ships similar to the *Cyclops*. After World War I, the navy had decommissioned the *Proteus* and the *Nereus* and sold them both to a Canadian shipping company. In the midst of World War II (1939–1945), the ships continued voyaging.

The *Proteus* left Saint Thomas, Virgin Islands, on November 23, 1941. It was headed for Portland, Maine. It carried 58 people and a load of bauxite intended for processing into aluminum.

The Sargasso Sea

The Sargasso Sea is part of the central gyre of the North Atlantic Ocean. A gyre is the point around which ocean currents circulate. The Sargasso Sea is bounded by four currents, including the Gulf Stream and the North Atlantic Currents, which are among the most powerful currents in the ocean. These currents cause the entire Sargasso Sea to rotate slowly clockwise. They also cause floating debris to accumulate in the gyre. Oceanographers recently discovered what has been called the North Atlantic Garbage Path in the Sargasso Sea, so named for the large amounts of debris found there.

This sea earned its name from the vast amounts of *Sargassum* seaweed it contains. In the centuries before motorized ships, sailors often worried their vessels would become entangled in the seaweed. As a result, the Sargasso Sea became the subject of many nautical horror stories.

Many sailing ships did stall in the Sargasso Sea. But seaweed was not the cause. The Sargasso Sea lies within a region called the Horse Latitudes. In this area, winds and currents are very calm. A ship dependent on its sails might stall in these calm waters for days—or even weeks.

Sometime after November 25, it vanished without a trace.

On December 10, the *Nereus* left the same port with the same load, bound for the same destination. After December 12, it too disappeared—along with its 61 crew members. Some blame storms or German torpedoes, but nothing has been proven.

Chapter 3

Looking Back on Flight 19

Disappearances had been happening off the southeastern coast of the United States since the mid-nineteenth century. But it was not until after Flight 19 that people started trying to connect the incidents.

Pondering the Sea's Puzzles

The US Navy had closed its books on Flight 19 in 1947. But a few years later, a newspaper article stirred up the embers of public interest.

On September 16, 1950, the Associated Press published an article by Edward Van Winkle Jones. The next day, the *Miami Herald* ran this article under the headline "Sea's Puzzles Still

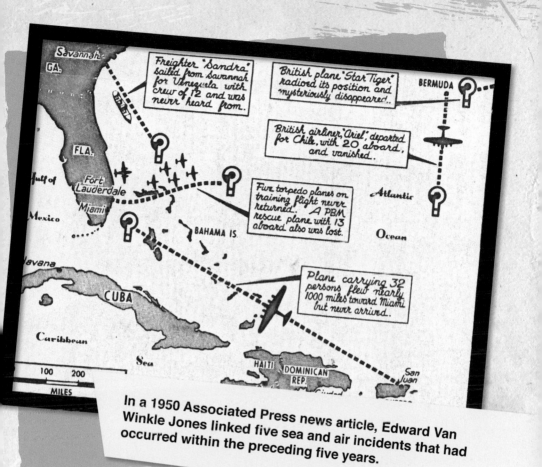

In a 1950 Associated Press news article, Edward Van Winkle Jones linked five sea and air incidents that had occurred within the preceding five years.

Baffle Men In Pushbutton Age." Jones describes a "misty limbo of the lost . . . into which a hundred and more persons have flown or sailed within brief memory, to be swallowed up just as ships were swallowed in the old sailing days."[1]

The article does not try to explain how this misty limbo swallows up ships and airplanes. Jones proposes no specific powers that might be at work there. Nor does he map the borders of this mysterious realm. In fact, he says it does not exist on any map. However, he does offer hints as to where a strange force might be active.

First Jones relates the story of the *Sandra*, a freighter that had disappeared earlier in 1950 somewhere between Savannah, Georgia, and Puerto Cabello, Venezuela. He says the *Sandra* measured 350 feet (107 m) and carried 12 men and 300 short tons (272 metric tons) of insecticide. He does not mention when the *Sandra* had departed, but notes that it had disappeared. He says searchers gave up looking for the ship on June 16.

Jones also describes the *Ariel*, an airliner that had vanished en route from Bermuda to Chile on January 18, 1949. He says a careful search by "thousands of pairs of sharp eyes" on "a great task force" of US Navy aircraft carriers, cruisers, and destroyers found no trace of the *Ariel* or of the 20 people it had carried.[2]

Jones tells of another airliner that had vanished on December 27, 1948, between

TUDOR IV AIRLINERS: The *Ariel* and the *Star Tiger* were both four-engine Tudor IV airliners owned by British South American Airways. After losing both the *Star Tiger* and the *Ariel*, British South American Airways withdrew all of its remaining Tudor IVs from passenger service.

San Juan, Puerto Rico, and Miami, Florida. He says the plane had last reported its position at 50 miles (80 km) south of Miami, but had never arrived—and could not be found.

Then Jones mentions the *Star Tiger*, yet another lost airliner. He says this plane and its 29 passengers had disappeared on January 31, 1948, on its way to Bermuda from the Azores.

Finally, Jones reminds readers about Flight 19. The fate of the missing planes was, he says, still a perplexing mystery:

> *They took off from the Navy's Fort Lauderdale air station on Dec. 5, 1945, for a navigational training flight. The hours passed and darkness fell. Anxious officers called to them by radio and were answered only with silence. The hour passed when their fuel would be exhausted and search planes were sent out. Among the searchers was a big, lumbering rescue craft, a PBM with 13 men on board. None of the five torpedo planes with the 14 crewmen were found despite the greatest search in Florida's history. Nor did the PBM rescue craft ever return.[3]*

Jones does not tell the whole story of Flight 19 in his brief newspaper article, but the statements he makes about this incident are essentially accurate. He offers no new evidence or ideas about the case.

Jones's article does do one new and important thing, though. It links Flight 19 to four other recent losses. In all five incidents, Jones says, people and the crafts that bore them had gone missing "without a trace."[4] By linking these incidents, he is implying that some harmful force was at work in the Atlantic Ocean.

A Fateful Story

Two years later, a popular magazine about the paranormal picked up the theme of Jones's article. In October 1952, *Fate* published a story by George X. Sand, "Sea Mystery at Our Back Door." Sand covers all the incidents Jones had mentioned. But Sand provides vivid details about each event.

In relating the 1950 *Sandra* incident, for example, Sand gives the same basic information about the ship and its crew, cargo, and route. He does not mention the dates of the *Sandra*'s trip or of the search effort. But he does describe the

FATE: *Fate* magazine is devoted to paranormal phenomena, or experiences that lie outside the range of normal experience or scientific explanation. Paranormal phenomena include ghosts, spirits, and demons; intelligent extraterrestrial life and unidentified flying objects (UFOs); and cryptids (animals unconfirmed by science, such as Bigfoot and the Loch Ness monster).

rust on the hull of the ship, the sights it passed along the Florida coast, and the actions and conversations of the crew as they enjoyed the "peaceful tropic dusk."[5]

Sand elaborates on the 1949 *Ariel* incident, too. He describes the airplane, names its captain and its company, and details its full itinerary from London to Bermuda to Jamaica to Chile. He shares the last

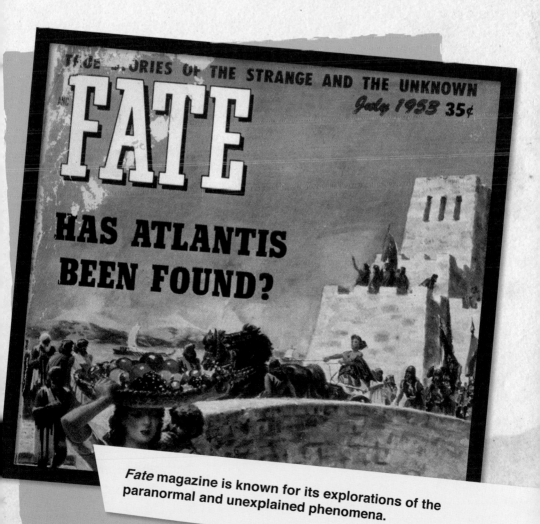

Fate magazine is known for its explorations of the paranormal and unexplained phenomena.

radio message received from the plane. He says the *Ariel* was flying at 300 miles per hour (483 km/h) when it vanished amid clear skies and calm seas. Then Sand echoes Jones's language in describing a

Comparing Stories

Sand's story of Flight 19 conflicts with the navy's report on several points:

George X. Sand	US Navy
Nobody heard from Flight 19 for hours after takeoff.	Flight 19 took off at 2:10 p.m. Cox heard from them at 4:00 p.m.
Flight 19 gave its position by radio at 5:25 p.m.	Flight 19 did not know its location. At 6:00 p.m. the navy calculated Flight 19's 5:50 p.m. location.
Nobody heard from Flight 19 after 5:25 p.m.	Navy personnel received many radio transmissions from Flight 19 between 4:00 p.m. and 7:04 p.m.
The navy launched a search after realizing Flight 19 must be out of gas.	Cox searched for Flight 19 beginning at approximately 4:00 p.m. The first flying boat took off at 6:20 p.m. Gas would run out at 7:30 p.m.–8:00 p.m.
Avengers were known for their buoyancy.	Avengers were heavy and would sink quickly.
The PBM disappeared without a trace.	*Gaines Mills* saw an explosion, debris, and oil. *Solomons* watched the PBM go off radar at the explosion site.
Nobody searching the PBM loss site found wreckage or oil the next morning.	The next day, water samples from the area contained oil.

"large task force" made up of "thousands of pairs of sharp eyes, trained for just such work," as they "scanned the surface of the smiling sea" in vain.[6]

Sand uses the same strategy as he explains the 1948 airliner loss near Miami and the *Star Tiger* incident. He relates the same basic information Jones had given, but supplements it with colorful details about the weather and the crafts and people involved.

Sand also describes one additional incident Jones had not mentioned. Sand says that in March 1948, famous horse racing jockey Al Snider had taken a cabin cruiser out of Miami on a fishing trip with two friends. They anchored the cruiser at Sandy Key, then launched a small fishing skiff. They never returned to the cruiser. Sand describes a search effort involving more than 800 people on land, in the air, and on the sea. Searchers found the skiff but never found the men.

A New View of Flight 19

Sand's description of Flight 19 is riveting. Sand says that for hours after the Avengers took off from Fort Lauderdale, "anxious buddies . . . listened in" on the radio, hoping in vain to hear from Flight 19.[7] At 5:25 p.m., a "routine message" from the Avengers had given their position.[8] Sand says this was the last anyone heard from Flight 19.

When the navy realized Flight 19 must have run out of gas, Sand writes, it launched a massive search. Meanwhile, Sand claims naval officials said Avengers were known for their buoyancy. Sand points out: "In similar emergencies such planes had always remained afloat long enough for the crews to launch the life rafts, often 'without even getting their feet wet.'"[9]

Sand describes the huge Martin Mariner PBM bomber that took 13 men to search for the missing

Many wrecks have been found off the coast of Bermuda, but not Flight 19.

Avengers. He writes dramatically, "*This plane, too, was to disappear without a trace.*"[10]

Flight 19 soon became the talk of the nation, Sand says. People wanted to know why the planes had disappeared. The Avengers could not all have collided in midair. And what about the Mariner? Sand notes that the *Gaines Mills* had reported an explosion in the sky at 7:50 p.m. But, he says, when planes and boats searched the area the next morning, they found no wreckage or oil.

Sand seemed to have found information that had not previously been known. Several of his statements, such as his comments about the buoyancy of Avengers, conflict with earlier reports. Was Sand making stuff up? Or was the navy hiding something?

"Sea Mystery at Our Back Door" renewed public interest in several tragic incidents by providing juicy details about the events. It also mapped a specific zone of danger in the North Atlantic.

Sand was the first writer to describe the triangular region familiar to modern readers. He did not name this danger zone. He simply said it was "a watery triangle bounded roughly by Florida, Bermuda and Puerto Rico" whose "potential for mystery apparently remains just as great today as when Columbus first sailed its milk-green waters."[11]

Chapter 4

Weaving a Web of Mystery

Jones's and Sand's articles got ordinary people thinking about ships and airplanes lost in the Atlantic Ocean. Both writers suggest a mysterious and hazardous force lurked there. Sand draws the boundaries of the danger zone, giving it a triangular shape. And by describing Flight 19 differently than the navy had, Sand opened the door to alternative explanations. Some people may have wondered which account was true. Others may not have known about the naval report and simply took Sand at his word.

The Deadly Triangle

Throughout the 1950s, Americans referred to "the
Triangle" when discussing boats or planes that
crashed or got lost in the North Atlantic. By the early
1960s, people were calling it the "Deadly Triangle."
In that decade, more writers began fueling the public
curiosity Jones and Sand had sparked.

A piece entitled "The Mystery of the Lost Patrol"
by Allan W. Eckert ran in the April 1962 issue of

The "Deadly Triangle" loomed large in travelers'
imaginations during the 1960s.

American Legion magazine. This story introduces several new ideas. It calls Flight 19 a patrol instead of a training flight. It also provides dialogue that had never before seen print. For example, Eckert writes that Taylor radioed, "We are entering white water, nothing seems right. We don't know where we are."[1] Other dialogue from Flight 19 says all the compasses were going haywire and the fliers could not make out any direction. Eckert also claims navy officials said the planes had flown "off to Mars."[2] His dialogue suggests that an electromagnetic—or extraterrestrial—phenomenon was involved in Flight 19's disappearance.

WINGS OF MYSTERY: In his 1962 book *Wings of Mystery: True Stories of Aviation History*, Dale Titler included a chapter titled "The Mystery of Flight 19." This chapter discusses not only Flight 19 but also other recent losses in the Bermuda Triangle. Like Eckert's article, Titler's book proposes that travelers in the Bermuda Triangle encountered strange electromagnetic conditions.

The Bermuda Triangle

In February 1964, the popular magazine *Argosy* published a piece by Vincent Gaddis called "The Deadly Bermuda Triangle." Gaddis spends approximately one-third of this long article discussing Flight 19.

In his description of Flight 19, Gaddis borrows ideas and wording from earlier writers. He calls the group a "routine patrol flight."[3] He includes similar dialogue: "We don't know which way is west. Everything is wrong . . . strange. We can't be sure of any direction. *Even the ocean doesn't look as it should.*"[4] According to Gaddis, the navy sent a "huge" Martin Mariner to help, meanwhile saying the Avengers would float long enough for the men to launch life rafts.[5] The fliers "shouldn't even get their feet wet."[6] Later, a naval official said Flight 19 and the Mariner "vanished as completely as if they had flown to Mars."[7]

Vincent Gaddis and *Argosy*

Vincent Gaddis gained fame as a freelance fiction writer. He wrote many mystery and adventure stories on paranormal topics. These stories appeared in full-length books and in pulp magazines (cheaply produced fiction magazines) and magazines devoted to the paranormal, such as *Fate* and *Argosy*.

Argosy was an old and well-known fiction magazine. It had been around since 1882. In the 1940s, it began changing slowly into a men's adventure magazine. In the 1960s, it was publishing a mix of fiction and nonfiction. The two genres were sometimes hard to distinguish in *Argosy*. Its science editor, Ivan T. Sanderson, was a famous biologist interested in the paranormal.

Argosy published stories in many genres from its founding in 1882.

Gaddis offers a new timeline of events for the incident. He says the flight of Avengers took off at 2:02 p.m. and was meant to last two hours.

The first radio message from Taylor was a distress call at 3:45 p.m. Taylor's and the students' voices were bewildered, then fearful, then hysterical. The last radio transmission from Flight 19 came in at 4:25 p.m. The Mariner took off immediately on its rescue mission, only to send "several routine radio reports" before vanishing itself.[8] The *Gaines Mills* witnessed an explosion in the sky at 7:30 p.m., but no one found wreckage or oil at the location. And instead of linking the explosion with the missing Mariner, Gaddis mentions the five missing Avengers. He writes, "The explosion occurred more than three hours after the last radio message from the patrol, and it is unlikely that there is a connection."[9]

The rest of "The Deadly Bermuda Triangle" describes 23 other boat and airplane losses in the North Atlantic, plus one airplane loss in Chile. Gaddis relates incidents as long ago as 1492 and as recent as 1963, including the stories of Al Snider (1948), the airliner lost near Miami (1948), and the *Sandra* (1950). He connects a large number of incidents in a way no previous writer did, implying they were all somehow related. He suggests atmospheric or magnetic aberrations may have caused many of the incidents.

But Gaddis seems unconvinced by such explanations. Several times, he repeats the idea that an unexplained menace lurked in the North Atlantic. He not only maps the location of this menace but also gives it a name: "Draw a line from Florida to Bermuda, another from Bermuda to Puerto Rico, and a third line back to Florida through the Bahamas. Within this area, known as the 'Bermuda Triangle,' most of the total vanishments have occurred."[10]

One year after Gaddis's article appeared in *Argosy*, it reappeared as a chapter in a book by Gaddis titled *Invisible Horizons*. Thanks to this exposure, the name *Bermuda Triangle* caught the public imagination, and the concept spread rapidly.

Spotlight on the Bermuda Triangle

Interest in the Bermuda Triangle exploded in the late 1960s and the 1970s. The first full-length book devoted to the Bermuda Triangle, *Limbo of the Lost* by John Spencer, was published in 1969. Spencer describes dozens of incidents in great detail,

LIMBO OF THE LOST: In 1973 and again in 1975, Spencer released updated and expanded editions titled *Limbo of the Lost—Today*. These new editions fueled the fire of public interest in the Bermuda Triangle.

including as many facts as possible about each loss and the ensuing search. He writes with a serious—not sensational—tone. But his opinion is obvious: He believes unidentified flying objects (UFOs) were responsible for all the Bermuda Triangle's losses. Dozens of newspaper and magazine articles followed in the 1970s.

The Bermuda Triangle stole the media spotlight in 1974. That year Richard Winer published a book called *The Devil's Triangle* and released a documentary film with the same title. Both describe incidents in the Bermuda Triangle with great detail but without sensationalism or paranormal theories. According to one reviewer, Winer "always makes an effort to point out possible natural explanations, even in cases where such explanations admittedly seem unlikely."[11]

The author who did the most to launch the Bermuda Triangle into popular culture was Charles Berlitz. In 1974, he published a book titled simply *The Bermuda Triangle*. In this book, Berlitz elaborates on his belief "that something is very wrong with this area."[12] He proposes several unusual theories to explain losses in the Bermuda Triangle, such as alien kidnappings, gravitational warps, magnetic aberrations, and technology left over from ancient lost civilizations.

Berlitz's dramatic storytelling and fascinating explanations grabbed the public imagination. Berlitz also had a famous name, a respectable background, and well-established media connections. He was a respected linguist and a member of the renowned Berlitz family, who had founded the Berlitz language schools and publishing company. *The Bermuda Triangle* became a best seller. It sold more than 500,000 copies in hardcover and many millions more in paperback.

Four years after *The Bermuda Triangle*'s release, a dramatic film based on this book—also called *The Bermuda Triangle*—hit movie theaters. It boasts John Huston, a big-name star, in a leading role. By the late 1970s, the Bermuda Triangle was one of the cultural talking points of the nation.

The Bermuda Triangle movie poster included the cover of the best-selling book. The movie helped keep the Bermuda Triangle in the public eye.

Chapter 5

Blame It on Aliens

As interest in the Bermuda Triangle grew, people proposed many theories to explain the losses experienced there. Some believed creatures from outer space or undersea were responsible. Others pointed to relics of ancient civilizations. Some suggested that mysterious forces were at work within the Bermuda Triangle. Still others suspected secret human activities were to blame.

Monsters and Aliens

Throughout the ages, humans have noted the ocean's power and peril. Mariners and landlubbers alike have woven tales of danger

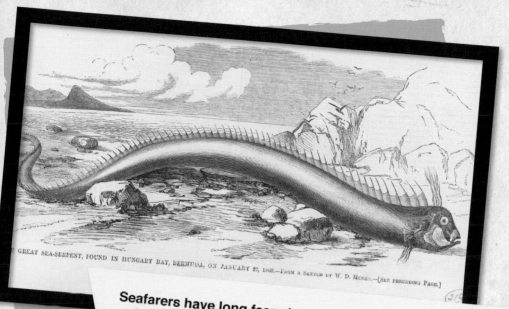

GREAT SEA-SERPENT, FOUND IN HUNGARY BAY, BERMUDA, ON JANUARY 22, 1860.—FROM A SKETCH BY W. D. MUNRO.—[SEE PRECEDING PAGE.]

Seafarers have long feared the existence of unknown monsters.

and mystery about the sea. Among these are many tales describing creatures—from mermaids to sea monsters to giant squids—that lured or dragged vessels to their doom. Many authors drew upon these tales to explain losses in the Bermuda Triangle. For example, Winer suggests huge, scary creatures might exist in the Bermuda Triangle. In *The Devil's Triangle* he describes an underwater filming encounter with a creature "maybe a hundred feet across. . . . It was perfectly round. Its color was a deep purple. It was moving slowly up toward us. At its outer perimeter there was a form of pulsation, but there was no movement of water. As we started for the surface, it stopped its ascent. Then slowly it began to descend into the blackening depths."[1]

In *Limbo of the Lost*, Spencer strongly believes alien scientists are taking samples of humans and human technology in order to learn about us. According to Spencer, aliens "clearly do not want to socialize or fraternize with earth beings," so they build "their bases and laboratory facilities deep under the ocean . . . whenever they need someone or something for experimental purposes, all they have to do is leave their facilities, take what they want, and return to their hidden underwater laboratories."[2] He claims that a relationship exists between frequent UFO sightings and disappearances in the Bermuda Triangle.

UFOS: Many UFO sightings have been reported from the Bahamas. Some people believe these sightings are related to ship and airplane losses in the area.

In *The Bermuda Triangle*, Berlitz agrees with Spencer. He claims that "extraterrestrials periodically visit the earth and kidnap or 'spacenap' men and equipment" for research purposes.[3] He suggests that these beings might come directly from outer space, they might be forms of intelligent life living below Earth's oceans, or they might come from another dimension rather than another place.

The Legacy of Atlantis

Atlantis is a legendary island civilization. The writings of the ancient Greek scholar Plato contain the earliest surviving description of Atlantis. He calls it a "great and wonderful empire."[4] In the legend, it lay in the Atlantic Ocean and had a strong navy, which conquered many parts of Europe and Africa in the 9000s BCE. Atlantis tried to conquer the Greek city-state of Athens, but failed.

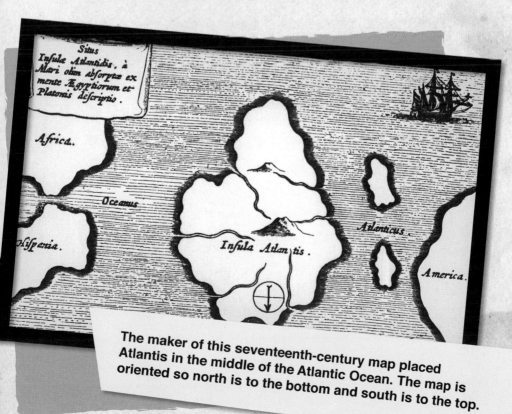

The maker of this seventeenth-century map placed Atlantis in the middle of the Atlantic Ocean. The map is oriented so north is to the bottom and south is to the top.

Divers swim over the seafloor formation known as the Bimini Road. It is sometimes associated with Atlantis although it likely occurred naturally.

After this failure, writes Plato, "there occurred violent earthquakes and floods; and in a single day and night of misfortune all [Atlantis's] warlike men in a body sank into the earth, and the island of Atlantis in like manner disappeared in the depths of the sea. For which reason the sea in those parts is impassable and impenetrable. . . ."[5]

Later writers built upon Plato's story of Atlantis. They expanded it and embroidered it with details. Many cast Atlantis as a utopian society. Some said that Atlantis possessed advanced technologies.

In modern times, some authors who wrote about the Bermuda Triangle drew connections between the Bermuda Triangle and Atlantis. They claimed Atlantis lay within the Bermuda Triangle and that remnants of its technology caused ships and planes to vanish.

Edgar Cayce, a famous psychic,

Bimini Road

Cayce predicted that in 1968 or 1969, the western edge of Atlantis would be discovered near the coast of Bimini, a chain of small islands in the western Bahamas approximately 53 miles (85 km) east of Miami, Florida.

In 1968, a researcher found an unusual rock formation there, something that looked like an underwater road. It was made up of stone blocks measuring an average of six to nine feet (2 to 3 m). The blocks had rounded corners and looked like giant loaves of bread.

Other divers and researchers soon explored the area. They determined the formation was approximately 0.5 miles (0.8 km) long. They called it the Bimini Road or Bimini Wall. They also discovered two smaller, similar formations nearby.

The rock is a type of limestone called beach rock, which occurs naturally and is common in the area. Some people believed the formations were not formations at all, but human-made structures left over from an ancient civilization. They claimed the discovery of the Bimini Road fulfilled Cayce's prediction—and therefore proved the ruins of Atlantis must lie within the Bermuda Triangle, causing the odd happenings there.

believed the citizens of Atlantis had developed a special crystal that could collect vast amounts of energy from various elements and phenomena in nature. He said the Atlanteans used this crystal as a power source. He claimed this crystal caused the destruction of Atlantis and that it sank along with its creators to the bottom of the ocean.

According to Berlitz, this crystal survived when Atlantis sank. He wrote that it continued to function, occasionally releasing its energy and "causing electromagnetic stresses or drains resulting in the malfunctioning or disintegration of sea and air craft."[6]

Mysterious Forces

Most authors who wrote about the Bermuda Triangle in the 1960s and 1970s suggest mysterious forces might be operating there. In "The Mystery of the Lost Patrol," Eckert describes an unstable atmospheric aberration or "temporal aberration."[7] He says that unusual electromagnetic or gravitational currents in the Bermuda Triangle carry planes and boats into alternate dimensions of space and time.

Gaddis echoed these ideas in "The Deadly Bermuda Triangle." He suggests that "an unknown type of atmospheric aberration . . . called 'a hole in the sky'" might be to blame.[8] Although Gaddis does not explain why this aberration exists or how it works, he insists that "many commercial pilots who fly the triangle take the aberration theory seriously. How else, they ask, can you explain what has been happening?"[9]

COLUMBUS'S LUMINOUS WATER:
In 1492, as Christopher Columbus sailed across the Atlantic Ocean from Europe to the Americas, he noted an eerie light in the water around his ships. He described this luminous water in his ship's log. Like other sailors of the time, Columbus and his crew believed sea monsters or mysterious forces caused the ocean to glow.

In *The Bermuda Triangle*, Berlitz reinforces and expands these concepts. He proposes that antimatter exists in the Bermuda Triangle. He also expresses puzzlement over glowing streaks and wheels of water present there. He calls these phenomena a "baffling mystery" and blames them on unseen forces beneath the sea.[10]

Conspiracy Theories

Some authors did not find it necessary to blame the Bermuda Triangle's losses on aliens, monsters, ancient civilizations, or unexplained energies. They blamed humans.

In *Wings of Mystery*, Titler suggests that electromagnetic anomalies could be causing aircraft to disappear in the Bermuda Triangle. He implies

ANTIMATTER: Antimatter is matter with properties exactly the opposite of matter. Some scientists believe antimatter may once have existed or may still exist somewhere in the universe. If matter and antimatter meet, they explode and neutralize each other. Some theorists believe the Bermuda Triangle contains antimatter.

Project Magnet might be involved. Project Magnet was a Canadian Department of Transport research program examining the possibility of using Earth's magnetic field as a source of propulsion. Project Magnet also investigated UFO reports. The program's director believed that humans could learn about magnetic propulsion by studying the movements of UFOs.

Some people thought the United States was to blame. They believed dangerous research and testing was under way at the Atlantic Undersea Test and Evaluation Center (AUTEC), a facility on Andros Island in the Bahamas. The US Navy built AUTEC in 1964 and currently uses it to test submarines, sonar, sensors, and weapons. A few theorists insisted the US government had been working with extraterrestrials and that AUTEC is actually a testing ground for Earth-adapted alien technology.

JUNE

25 CENTS
IN CANADA 30 CENTS

AMAZING STORIES

*Scientifiction
Stories by*

A. Hyatt Verrill
John W. Campbell, Jr.
Edmond Hamilton

This magazine featured a story about mysterious forces at work in the Bermuda Triangle.

Chapter 6

Some Facts Are Hard to Ignore

In the 1970s, several authors promoted the mystery of the Bermuda Triangle. Interest in the topic was ablaze, and their books and movies reached millions of people. Meanwhile, other authors questioned the fantastic claims being made about the Bermuda Triangle. These authors had much smaller audiences, but they asked questions and pointed out facts that were hard to ignore.

Michael McDonell: "Lost Patrol"

Michael McDonell served as an officer in the US Marine Corps in Vietnam from 1967 to 1968. After his tour of duty, he returned to the United States and became a professional writer.

While McDonell was starting his career, US society was growing enthralled with "unexplained" phenomena such as the Bermuda Triangle.

McDonell felt something was not quite right about the Bermuda Triangle mystery. So in 1973, he researched and wrote an article titled "Lost Patrol" about Flight 19 for *Naval Aviation News*. He notes that this incident is the central element in most accounts of the Bermuda Triangle. He tries to sort the facts of Flight 19 from the fiction. "It is this writer's view that many a good tale would lie a-dying if all the facts were included," he explained.[1]

First he retells the popular Flight 19 story. It goes roughly as follows.

Five Avengers take off at 2:00 p.m. They are flying a patrol east of Fort Lauderdale, scheduled to take two hours. The five pilots are highly experienced, and all the planes were checked carefully before the mission. They are expecting a beautiful, sunny day.

AN UNDERSTANDABLE FASCINATION: McDonell understood why Americans found stories about the Bermuda Triangle so fascinating. "There is something oddly provoking about these occurrences," he admitted, "particularly the 'normal' circumstances which existed prior to each disaster."[2]

At 3:45 p.m., the flight leader calls the tower at Fort Lauderdale. Sounding worried and confused, he says, "Cannot see land. . . . We seem to be off course." [3]

The tower asks for their position. Tower personnel look for the planes approaching the airport, but see nothing.

"We cannot be sure where we are," continues the flight leader. "Repeat: Cannot see land." [4]

Ten minutes later, the tower hears the voices of the crews. They sound confused and disoriented.

This airplane disappeared with the lost patrol. The men shown were not Flight 19 crew members.

"We can't find west. Everything is wrong. We can't be sure of any direction. Everything looks strange, even the ocean." [5] For an unknown reason, a different pilot appeared to have taken over command of the flight.

Twenty minutes pass before the new flight leader contacts the control tower again. Now he sounds very upset. "We can't make out anything. We think we may be about 225 miles northeast of base. . . . It looks like we are entering white water. We're completely lost." [6] This was the last message from Flight 19.

A Mariner flying boat takes off minutes later on the rescue mission. It radios in to the tower once and then disappears forever. For five days, ships and planes search 250,000 square miles (650,000 sq km) of the Atlantic Ocean and the Gulf of Mexico. They find a calm sea, clear skies, and middling winds—and nothing else.

A navy investigation fails to find a cause for the disappearances. The report concludes, "We are not able to even make a good guess as to what happened." [7]

Then McDonell examines this story. First, he notes that the books and articles relating this popular story "bear striking resemblances to one another." [8] They share recurring passages of dialogue and description. These recurring passages suggest either that the pieces borrowed heavily from one another or that they all relied upon the same original source, says McDonell.

Next, he compares the details of the popular story with the facts recorded in the Navy Board of Investigation's report. This report includes radio logs, witness testimonies, and expert opinions. McDonell notes the following contradictions:

1. Flight 19 was not a two-hour patrol; it was a three-hour training exercise in navigation and low-level bombing.

2. The five pilots had varying amounts of experience. They included four students and one instructor. The students were relatively inexperienced. The instructor was highly experienced but had never flown this exercise before.

3. The planes were thoroughly checked, but none of them had a clock.

4. There was no "excellent" weather report. The flight had not received an unfavorable weather report and presumed the weather to be favorable. Seas were reported moderate to rough.

5. The Fort Lauderdale tower did not receive a distress call from Flight 19 at 3:45 p.m. At that time, a different instructor flying over Fort Lauderdale overheard a conversation among the Flight 19 pilots indicating they had gotten lost.

6. Flight 19 did not know its position. The instructor thought Flight 19 was over the

Navigation Tools

In the 1940s, an airplane pilot could use several tools and methods to determine position and plan a course. A pilot could observe features on Earth's surface or celestial bodies such as the sun, stars, and moon. A magnetic compass could show direction. Radio and radar could help a pilot determine both direction and location. A clock was useful, too. It could help a pilot determine the distance traveled at a certain speed over a specific time. In addition, navigating by the stars requires the pilot know accurately what time it is.

It was important for pilots to have a variety of navigational tools and methods in case one or more became unusable. For example, a pilot's compass, radio, or radar might fail. In bad weather or in darkness, a pilot might not be able to see celestial bodies or terrestrial features.

Gulf of Mexico. The students thought they were over the Atlantic Ocean. They never agreed on their location or received information about it.

7. The navy did not wait until it lost contact with Flight 19 to launch a search effort. Navy personnel sprang into action immediately after hearing the first radio transmission. The effort to locate Flight 19 included several land-based radio and radar stations, all ships in the area, and at least four airplanes dispatched to find Flight 19. The popular story omits all of these efforts and many exchanges between Flight 19 and navy personnel.

8. The navy did not lose contact with Flight 19 around 4:30 p.m.; it was still receiving garbled messages after 6:20 p.m.

9. The search effort did not encounter calm

More Discrepancies

In addition to the discrepancies explained by McDonell, a careful reader will note a few additional problems with the popular tale. For example, none of the dialogue in the popular story appears in the radio logs. In addition, no radio transmissions from Flight 19 indicated terror or hysteria. A few were terse and irritated, but all were calm. Finally, the navy's original report did find pilot error a factor in the Flight 19 disappearance, but the final report was changed at the insistence of the flight commander's family.

seas and clear skies. Witnesses reported high winds, high seas, rain, a low ceiling of clouds, and darkness.

10. One of the Mariner planes sent out to search for Flight 19 was unaccounted for shortly after takeoff. The search effort did find some evidence of the Mariner's fate: an oil slick and debris. The debris could not be retrieved because the sea was too turbulent.

11. Navy opined that the Mariner had caught fire, crashed, and exploded in the sea at a specific location.

McDonell notes that the final navy report does not identify a cause for the loss of Flight 19. But he uses the evidence in the report to arrive at a conclusion of his own.

McDonell deduces that the instructor and students were struggling to decide whether they were over the Atlantic or the Gulf. As they changed their minds and their course, they "zigzagged through the area north of the Bahamas."[9] Meanwhile, the weather turned nasty, night fell, and the Avengers ran out of gas. "They descended through the dark toward a foaming, raging sea. . . . The aircraft most probably broke up on impact and those crewmen who might have survived the crash would not have lasted long."[10]

McDonell admits his conclusion was an educated guess. But because his guess was based on primary evidence and the opinions of former Avenger pilots, he feels confident that it was the most likely explanation.

Howard Rosenberg: "Exorcizing the Devil's Triangle"

Howard Rosenberg wrote for the navy's *Sealift* magazine. Similar to McDonell, Rosenberg wondered about all the stories promoting the mystery of the Bermuda Triangle. In a 1974 *Sealift* article titled "Exorcizing the Devil's Triangle," he writes, "There supposedly is some inexplicable force within it that causes ships and planes to vanish. . . . Few have really dug into all the aspects of this mystery, but many are content to attribute the loss of Flight 19 to some mysterious source."[11]

Rosenberg commends McDonell for his digging into the Flight 19 incident. And he agrees with McDonell's observations and conclusions. He also mentions a few of the other incidents typically included in the Bermuda Triangle mystery, such as the loss of the *Cyclops*.

Rosenberg understands that humans are storytellers. And he notes that when natural explanations are difficult to come by, humans turn to the supernatural. "But," he says, "it is amazing how many supernatural things become natural when scientifically investigated."[12]

Rosenberg goes on to describe several natural forces at work in the Bermuda Triangle. Any of these forces, he says, could bring down a plane or sink a ship.

First he points out that the Bermuda Triangle was known for its unpredictable weather. He quotes meteorologists who explained that small, violent thunderstorms could occur at sea with little or no warning and then dissipate quickly. Their electric activity could foul up communication systems. Such storms were especially common and especially violent over the Gulf Stream. Some storms formed waterspouts, which could "wreck almost anything."[13]

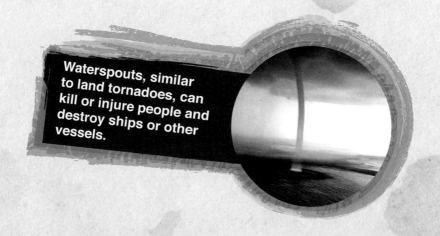

Waterspouts, similar to land tornadoes, can kill or injure people and destroy ships or other vessels.

Rosenberg also draws on the Coast Guard's knowledge and experience. He quotes a retired Coast Guard captain, who pointed out that many travelers through the area did not understand the Gulf Stream. "When it collides with strong northeast winds, extremely stiff seas build up. . . . The waves break and you get a vertical wall of water from 30 to 40 feet [9 to 12 m] high coming down on you."[14]

Rosenberg notes that the Coast Guard had answered approximately 8,000 distress calls in the area during the preceding year. Most calls resulted from human error. Boaters and pilots often made mistakes due to inexperience, poor planning, and lack of caution. The single biggest problem was running out of gas.

Rosenberg also describes the seafloor in the Bermuda Triangle. Near the US coast it is only 50–100 feet (15–30 m) deep, but most of the area is approximately 19,000 feet (5,791 m) deep. The Bermuda Triangle includes the Atlantic's deepest trench, the Puerto Rico Trench, which drops to 27,500 feet (8,382 m).

Rosenberg's weather and seafloor observations explain the lack of evidence left by losses in the Bermuda Triangle. Because the Gulf Stream is so strong, it disperses debris quickly. And because the sea is so deep, sunken crafts are very difficult to find.

The Bermuda Triangle is one of the most heavily traveled areas in the world, he says. Heavy traffic plus multiple natural hazards equals a high chance of accidents. As for all the supernatural theories: Rosenberg concludes they "amount to a voluminous mass of sheer hokum."[15]

Gulf Stream

The Gulf Stream is a strong ocean current that flows northward along the western part of the Bermuda Triangle. It behaves similarly to a river within the ocean. It begins in the western Caribbean Sea and flows northward along the eastern coast of North America at 2 to 5 miles per hour (3 to 8 km/h). It is part of the North Atlantic gyre, a large circular system of currents that moves water clockwise around the North Atlantic Ocean. The Gulf Stream moves approximately 140 million short tons (127 million metric tons) of water per second at its widest and deepest point. Its flow is approximately 500 times the flow of the Amazon River.

Chapter 7

A Mystery Solved?

In the early 1970s, Larry Kusche was working as a reference librarian at Arizona State University. He was getting a lot of requests for information on the Bermuda Triangle. It seemed everyone wanted to know more about the mystery.

Kusche found very few materials at first. So he teamed up with colleague Deborah Blouin, and together they asked government agencies, libraries, and organizations around the country to suggest resources on the Bermuda Triangle. Kusche and Blouin compiled a long bibliography on the subject.

But Kusche still was not satisfied. The suggested resources were hard to locate. And when he read the materials, he found

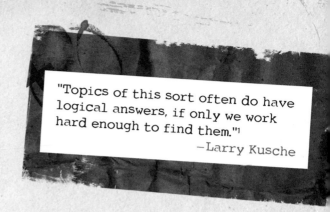

"Topics of this sort often do have logical answers, if only we work hard enough to find them."[1]
—Larry Kusche

they provided few hard facts about the Bermuda Triangle. Kusche happened to be an experienced pilot. The materials he found made claims that did not mesh well with his knowledge of navigation, weather, and other related facts.

So Kusche set out to find more resources. He pored over old newspapers and insurance records. He consulted with experts in aviation, shipping, meteorology, oceanography, history, navigation, and other fields related to losses in the Bermuda Triangle. He read hundreds of military records and weather reports. In 1975 he published all this research in a book titled *The Bermuda Triangle Mystery—Solved.*

Examining the Incidents

In his book, Kusche investigates more than 50 incidents commonly mentioned in conjunction with the Bermuda Triangle. These incidents stretched from Columbus's 1492 expedition to the disappearance of an American fishing boat called the *Linda* in 1973.

Kusche devotes one chapter to each incident. In each chapter, he first describes the popular version of the event. Then he shares and explains excerpts from primary sources that reported on the incident. Finally, he offers his own opinion on the event. In some cases, Kusche could not find enough evidence to dispel the mystery. But in most cases, he found ample evidence to offer natural, logical explanations.

Kusche begins with the August 1840 *Rosalie* incident. He found the London *Times* newspaper that reported this event, but he could not find any others. He did, however, obtain helpful records from the international shipping journal *Lloyd's List* and from the Bahamian government. These records strongly suggest the *Times* got the ship's name wrong, and the *Rosalie* was actually the *Rossini*. The *Rossini* had run aground in the Bahama Channel. Another ship rescued the *Rossini*'s crew and passengers but left the ship behind. Later another ship found the deserted *Rossini*.

Kusche also investigates the *Cyclops*'s disappearance in March 1918. His research suggests the navy was looking for the *Cyclops* in the wrong place. Investigators assumed the ship had gone down soon after leaving Barbados. So they searched the southern part of the *Cyclops*'s route but not the northern part. By Kusche's calculations, if the *Cyclops* had run into trouble later in its trip, it would have been somewhere along the North Carolina or Virginia coast on March 9 or 10. On those two days, a severe storm battered the area. Kusche proposes that the storm's raging winds and high seas shifted the *Cyclops*'s heavy cargo, causing the ship to roll and sink without warning. To support his theory, Kusche notes that in 1968, navy diver Dean Hawes spotted a sunken wreck resembling the *Cyclops* near Norfolk, Virginia.

Lloyd's of London

Lloyd's of London is an organization that has its roots in the late seventeenth century at Lloyd's Coffee House in London. The coffee house was a popular meeting place for sailors, merchants, ship owners, and financial backers of shipping. Members of the shipping community frequented the place to keep up on shipping news and to discuss insurance deals among themselves. This community eventually organized into formal society and then into a financial market for insurance companies. Lloyd's of London is still active today. Throughout its long history, Lloyd's of London and related organizations, such as Lloyd's Register and the newspaper *Lloyd's List*, have served as the shipping industry's most comprehensive and reliable source of news.

Dean Hawes and the *Cyclops*

Hawes was looking for a missing submarine in 1968 when he found a sunken wreck resembling the *Cyclops*. He was impressed by the steel structures towering over the deck; he had never seen anything like them. He wanted to explore the wreck further, but bad weather intervened. Hawes thought little more about this wreck until several years later, when he read a story and saw a photo of the *Cyclops*. He persuaded the navy to investigate. In 1974, navy divers did so. They found another wreck, but it was not the ship Hawes had described.

When he researched the 1925 *Cotopaxi* incident, Kusche found a simple solution to the mystery of its disappearance. The popular story did not mention the weather along the *Cotopaxi*'s route. But weather reports were easy to find. On December 1, the day the ship told Florida radio operators that it was listing badly, all of Florida had suffered severe weather. The *New York Times* reported, "The storm was described by Weather Bureau observers as 'phenomenal.'"[2]

Kusche then shares the popular version of the 1941 *Proteus* and *Nereus* incidents. The story raises the possibility of bombing by German submarines—but dismisses this idea, saying that no subs had been reported in the area. Kusche finds no new evidence, but he sides with the US military.

The United States was just entering World War II, and both ships carried cargoes important to the US war effort. German torpedoes were the most likely culprits.

Kusche devotes his longest chapter to Flight 19. Over the course of 25 pages, he shares the full legend of Flight 19, reviews the navy's voluminous report on the incident, and analyzes both. He lists the many small problems that eventually led to a major disaster, from technical difficulties to bad weather and from human error to the military discipline that kept Flight 19 in step with its confused leader. In the end, Kusche agrees with the navy's assessment. The Avengers had to ditch in the Atlantic east of Florida sometime after 7:04 p.m. The bad weather, cold, high seas, and darkness made survival unlikely. The Mariner exploded at 7:50 p.m. in the sea east of New Smyrna Beach, Florida.

Kusche's Conclusions

After examining dozens of Bermuda Triangle incidents, Kusche arrived at several overall conclusions:

- Whenever he could find adequate information about an incident, he could usually also find a logical explanation.

- Disappearances occur not just in the Bermuda Triangle but in all parts of the ocean, and even over land.
- Some of the lost ships and planes passed through the region, but no one knows where they disappeared.
- In many cases, searchers had no idea where a craft had gone missing, and so they had to spread themselves thinly over a huge area.
- Many incidents were not considered mysterious when they happened. They only became mysterious later when Triangle writers found references to them.
- During many of the incidents, the weather was bad.
- Many incidents occurred late in the day or at night, making a visual search difficult or impossible until the next morning. Delays gave the sea many hours to disperse debris and survivors.
- Many popular Bermuda Triangle writers cited no original research and

TICKED OFF: Berlitz was so grateful for Kusche and Blouin's bibliography on the Bermuda Triangle that he praised their work in his own book. After Kusche published his own book, which used different sources and criticized earlier Bermuda Triangle writers, Berlitz was ticked off. He deleted his praise of Kusche from all following editions of *The Bermuda Triangle*.

borrowed from earlier writers, perpetuating mistakes and fabrications.

- Many popular writers withheld, ignored, or failed to search for information that offered logical, natural explanations.

Kusche believed the Bermuda Triangle mystery owed its existence to careless research and writing and the normal human delight in a good mystery. People heard stories about the Bermuda Triangle so many times that they believed they were true. "It's bunk," Kusche declared: "The Legend of the Bermuda Triangle is a manufactured mystery."[3]

Rough seas contributed to many Bermuda Triangle disappearances.

Chapter 8

The Bermuda Triangle Today

After the 1970s, Americans seemed to lose interest in "unexplained" phenomena such as the Bermuda Triangle. A few more Bermuda Triangle books came out, but the public paid little attention to them. Still, today the public remains fascinated with the Bermuda Triangle, fact or fiction, and it serves as a reminder of the mysteries that remain to be solved about the natural forces that govern our planet.

A Response to Kusche

Today, some people still wonder if a strange force lurks in the western North Atlantic. Gian J. Quasar is the most vocal modern Bermuda

Triangle theorist. He is especially critical of Kusche. Quasar uses his Web site and books to provide counterclaims to Kusche's conclusions.

In the case of the *Rosalie*, for example, Quasar claims the description of the *Rosalie* provided by the *Times* of London does not match the description of the *Rossini*. However, he does not provide or direct readers to either description so that they can compare for themselves.

Quasar disagrees with Kusche's conclusion about the *Cyclops*, too. Quasar concurs that a storm happened off the Carolinas, but he does not believe the *Cyclops* had reached that point in its journey when the storm occurred.

Gian Quasar

Very little information is available about Gian Quasar's identity or background. He calls himself, among other things, a "true skeptic." He defines skepticism as a double-edged sword: "One side does not allow us to believe everything off hand; the other does not let us necessarily dismiss anything off hand."[1]

Among the many Bermuda Triangle theories he discusses on his Web site and in his 2005 book *Into the Bermuda Triangle* are UFOs, electronic fogs, malfunctions in space and time, and Atlantis.

Quasar's publishing history demonstrates a taste for tales of mystery. He has published a number of books on unexplained phenomena, including several books on Bermuda Triangle topics and one on Bigfoot.

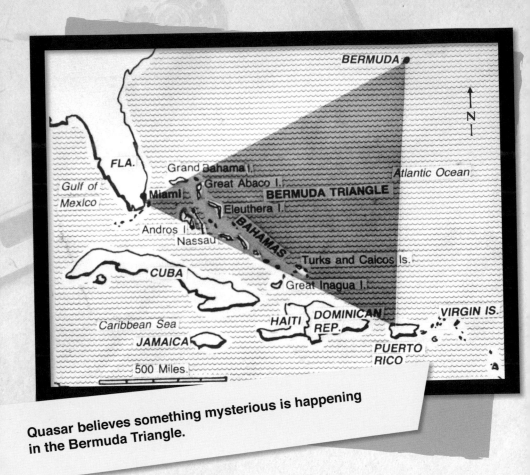

Quasar believes something mysterious is happening in the Bermuda Triangle.

Quasar also doubts that a storm caused the loss of the *Cotopaxi*. He says that, although newspapers reported a big storm, no official government records mention one. He points out that the *Cotopaxi* radioed its damaged condition after the alleged storm had passed the boat's location. Quasar suggests newspaper reports are not adequate proof of a storm and that the timing of *Cotopaxi*'s radio transmission indicates a different cause for its loss.

Quasar does not criticize Kusche's conclusion regarding the *Proteus* and *Nereus*. Quasar simply notes that Kusche agreed with the navy's assumption that German submarines were responsible for the losses.

Quasar criticizes Kusche's analysis of Flight 19 at great length. He claims Kusche did not understand naval aviation and had set out to prove his own theory rather than investigate the facts.

Generally speaking, Quasar says Kusche relies too heavily on contemporary news reports and does not dig deeply enough into government records. Quasar also says Kusche is too determined to find logical, natural explanations for Bermuda Triangle incidents. Quasar, by contrast, demonstrates an eagerness to maintain an air of mystery around the Bermuda Triangle.

"I see little difference between [Kusche's] credibility and those 'sensationalistic' accounts of UFOs kidnapping the pilots."[2]
—Gian Quasar

Meanwhile, Bermuda Triangle skeptics attempt to explain individual incidents there using the latest scientific knowledge. Modern scientists and officials in both civilian and military spheres tend to agree with Kusche. They say a variety of natural and human factors cause losses in the Bermuda Triangle.

Sea and Sky

The sea, sky, and undersea terrain within the Bermuda Triangle combine to form a treacherous area of ocean. Boaters and pilots traveling there face several natural dangers.

The region's seafloor varies from broad, shallow shoals and reefs to some of the world's deepest trenches. The western part of this seafloor lies beneath the wide, swift, and turbulent Gulf Stream. As the current roars through the area, it constantly changes the terrain and creates new navigational hazards.

The Gulf Stream carries huge amounts of warm tropical water northward along the western edge of the Bermuda Triangle. As it does so, it spawns high seas and intense weather patterns. The region is notorious for its violent waves, thunderstorms, waterspouts, and hurricanes.

In addition, when accidents

NO STORM WARNING: Before telegraph, radio, and radar were invented, sailors often did not know a storm was nearby until it appeared on the horizon. Although wave patterns and atmospheric conditions might hint of a brewing storm, sailors often lacked the tools to predict a storm's intensity with any accuracy.

happen within the Triangle, the people and vessels involved do not stay put. The Gulf Stream quickly carries off wreckage and bodies. Remnants not swept away sink to inaccessible depths.

At its other extreme, the parts of the Bermuda Triangle in the Horse Latitudes are calm and cloudy, confusing navigation and stranding ships that lack an internal power source. The region's sea and skies are unpredictable and intense. Many losses in the region leave no evidence behind. Together, these elements give the Bermuda Triangle an air of mystery.

Human Error

The Bermuda Triangle is a very busy area. It lies at a crossroads among continents. It encompasses busy trade routes and popular vacation spots. Every day, recreational boaters, cargo vessels, fishing boats, and cruise ships ply its waters. Private and commercial

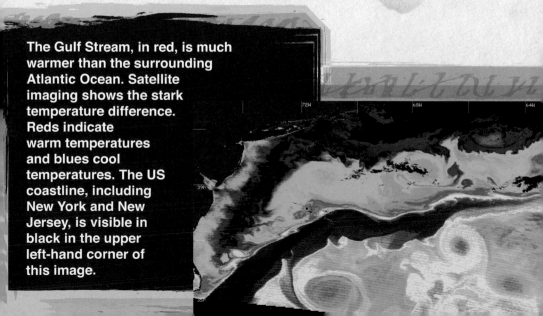

The Gulf Stream, in red, is much warmer than the surrounding Atlantic Ocean. Satellite imaging shows the stark temperature difference. Reds indicate warm temperatures and blues cool temperatures. The US coastline, including New York and New Jersey, is visible in black in the upper left-hand corner of this image.

Five Avengers Found

In May 1991, deep-sea explorer Graham Hawkes was searching for sunken ships. Instead, he discovered the wrecks of five Avenger bombers approximately 10 miles (16 km) off the coast of Fort Lauderdale. The planes all lay within an area approximately 1.4 miles (2.2 km) wide. They were sitting upright and showed little damage.

When Hawkes announced his find, many people believed the planes were the lost aircraft of Flight 19. One of the wrecks had the number *28* on its wing. This was the number of instructor Charles Taylor's plane. Two of the planes bore the letters *FT*. These letters designated their base as the Fort Lauderdale Naval Air Station.

But independent investigation revealed the aircraft had different serial numbers and were older Avenger models than those in Flight 19. It also showed the planes sank independently over several years.

airplanes large and small crisscross its skies.

Ship captains, recreational boaters, and airplane pilots of all kinds—regardless of their skill, knowledge, and experience levels—are human. Humans make mistakes. When human error meets bad weather, hazardous seas, or equipment failure, accidents happen.

In 2010 alone, the Coast Guard counted 4,604 accidents within its jurisdiction throughout US waters. It identified inattention, improper lookout, inexperience, excessive speed, and alcohol use as the top five causes of these accidents. A report published by the US Coast Guard explains that mistakes cause or contribute to the vast majority of accidents.

"Analysis indicates that human error is identified as a causal factor in 80 to 90 percent of mishaps and is present but not causal in another 50 to 60 percent of all mishaps, and is therefore the single greatest mishap hazard."[3]

The US Federal Aviation Administration (FAA) agrees with this analysis as it applies to airplane mishaps. In a safety publication aimed at general aviators (pilots flying noncommercial airplanes), the FAA reminds the public, "Pilot error causes more than 80 percent of aviation accidents."[4]

Underwater explorers found five wrecked Avenger airplanes on the seafloor in the Bermuda Triangle area, but they were not the Flight 19 planes.

For airplanes and ships alike, experts agree human error accounts for most accidents.

Deadly Bubbles

The seafloor off the southeastern coast of the United States contains large amounts of trapped frozen methane gas. The extreme cold and pressure turns the methane into an ice-like solid called gas hydrate.

An earthquake or underwater landslide may cause a portion of gas hydrate to break off from the seafloor and melt. When released, it rises toward the surface where it may become a giant bubble.

Researchers David May and Joseph Monaghan of Monash University in Melbourne, Australia, simulated and studied this phenomenon. They showed how a giant methane bubble can sink a boat. The bubble must be at least as wide as the boat is long, and the boat must be positioned between the rim and the center of the bubble. May and Monaghan found that when the bubble reached the surface, it formed a mound. The unluckily positioned boat slid down the mound, and then the bubble burst. "When the bubble burst, you got this high velocity jet of fluid spurting down into the water, pushing the boat under with it," explained May.[5]

Scientists agree that gas hydrates exist within the Bermuda Triangle. They also agree that a gas hydrate release can sink a ship. However, they caution there is no evidence of any recent eruptions in that part of the Atlantic Ocean. Bill Dillon, a geologist at the US Geological Survey's Woods Hole Science Center, believes that such a release last occurred at least 15,000 years ago.

Magnetic Variations

Many stories about Bermuda Triangle incidents include compass problems and the suggestion of magnetic anomalies. Some mention that the Bermuda Triangle is one of two places on Earth at which a magnetic compass points toward true north instead of magnetic north.

True north is toward the North Pole. Magnetic north is toward a point that varies with Earth's magnetic field, which is always in flux. The movement of this point is called polar wandering. The point is near, but not at, the North Pole. Therefore, the direction in which a compass points depends on where the compass is on Earth.

The difference between true north and magnetic north at any particular location is called magnetic variation. Pilots, boaters, trekkers, and navigators of all stripes know they must take

Electronic Fog

In 1970, Florida pilot Bruce Gernon and his father were flying from the Bahamas' Andros Island to Bimini Island when they saw a strange cloud ahead. They say it had almost perfectly round edges, and it grew as they tried to fly over it. Then it transformed into a tunnel. Gernon flew into it.

Gernon said the walls of the tunnel were spinning. His compass and his navigational instruments went haywire. When he exited the tunnel, he found himself in a gray haze. He contacted Miami Air Traffic Control, which told him no planes appeared on radar between Miami, Bimini, and Andros—but that the radar did show one plane over Miami.

Gernon said when the haze finally cleared, he was over Miami Beach. This was much farther than he could have traveled in the time that had elapsed. As a result, Gernon believed he had flown through an anomaly that allowed time travel.

Gernon believes that a rare natural phenomenon he calls "electronic fog" might lie behind many Bermuda Triangle incidents, causing time distortions, pilot disorientation, and equipment malfunctions. He explained his theory in a 2005 book titled The Fog.

magnetic variation into account. If they do not, they "can find themselves far off course and in deep trouble," a naval historian explained.[6] However, this is true anywhere on the planet—not only in the Bermuda Triangle.

For a time between the fifteenth and nineteenth centuries, true north and magnetic north were aligned in the area of the Bermuda Triangle. Some people even believed this alignment caused compasses to malfunction, but this is false. Today, magnetic north has moved and the line of alignment for magnetic and true north lies in the Gulf of Mexico.

An Unromantic Reality

Some people are convinced they have experienced unusual phenomena in the Bermuda Triangle. Others think it is important to keep their minds open to explanations beyond the bounds of science. They believe academic researchers might ignore evidence for fear of damaging their careers. Government officials might not tell the whole story because it is in their best interest to downplay suspicion. People who experience anomalies might keep them secret for fear of not being believed.

But most modern researchers say that, statistically speaking, the Bermuda Triangle is no

more dangerous than any other area of open ocean.
John Reilly of the US Naval Historical Foundation
quipped, "The region is highly traveled. . . . To say
quite a few ships and airplanes have gone down there
is like saying there are an awful lot of car accidents
on the New Jersey Turnpike."[7] In other words, the
Bermuda Triangle's mishaps occur in proportions
reasonable for the heavy traffic there. Skeptics find it
especially telling that members of Lloyd's of London
marine insurance market do not charge higher
rates for travel through the region, though they
charge higher rates in areas prone to piracy and in
war zones.

Neither the US Navy nor the Coast Guard
believes the Bermuda Triangle exists—not as
a mysterious, hazardous region, anyway. After
reviewing many ship and plane losses through
the years, the Coast Guard declared it had never
identified any extraordinary factors. Nature, human
error, equipment failure, and bad luck can explain
most losses.

Geologists, geographers, meteorologists,
oceanographers, and many other kinds of scientists
remain skeptical, too. They believe the evidence
reveals no real mystery. However, the excitement
surrounding the mystery does provide an important

clue about human nature. As Bill Norrington, a geographer at the University of California Santa Barbara, observed: "Myth, mystery, and miracle make for good press, and bad news certainly outsells good news. . . . The real mystery about the Bermuda Triangle isn't that much of a mystery—our love/hate obsession with the unknown is what defines us."[8]

DEDICATED TO ALL U.S. NAVAL AVIATORS
WHO SERVED AT NAVAL AIR STATION, FORT LAUDERDALE
(FT. LAUDERDALE – HOLLYWOOD INTERNATIONAL AIRPORT)
DURING WORLD WAR II

IN PARTICULAR

TO THOSE OFFICERS AND CREWMEN FLYING
FIVE NAVY AVENGER TORPEDO BOMBERS
FROM THIS NAVAL AIR STATION ON 5 DECEMBER 1945
WHO MYSTERIOUSLY DISAPPEARED IN WHAT HAS BECOME
KNOWN AS BERMUDA OR DEVIL'S TRIANGLE.

LT. CHARLES C. TAYLOR, COMMANDING

JOSEPH TIPTON BOSSI
ROBERT GALLIVAN
ROBERT GRUEBEL
GEORGE PAONESSA
GEORGE STIVERS
HERMAN THELANDER

GEORGE DEVLIN
FORREST J. GERBER
WILLIAM LIGHTFOOT
WALTER PARPART, JR.
EDWARD POWERS, JR.
HOWELL THOMPSON

BERT VALUK, JR.

DEDICATED BY
BROWARD COUNTY WOMENS COUNCIL NAVY LEAGUE OF UNITED STATES
1971

A plaque in Fort Lauderdale commemorates the men who disappeared with Flight 19.

Tools and Clues

bad weather– The seas of the Bermuda Triangle are known for sudden storms, which account for many of the disappearances in the region.

bioluminescence– Throughout history, mariners have reported streaks, wheels, or patches of glowing water within the Bermuda Triangle. Some theorists believe such light is evidence of a strange force lurking there; scientists believe it is simply bioluminescence.

craft design– Several disappearances can be attributed in part to the design of the vehicle itself. Avenger aircraft are known to sink rapidly. Top-heavy vessels such as the *Cyclops* can easily sink in rough waters.

disappearances– Throughout history, many ships and planes have been lost in the area of the Bermuda Triangle and their wreckage never found. Although most experts say these losses are statistically probable, others theorize mysterious forces are at work in the area.

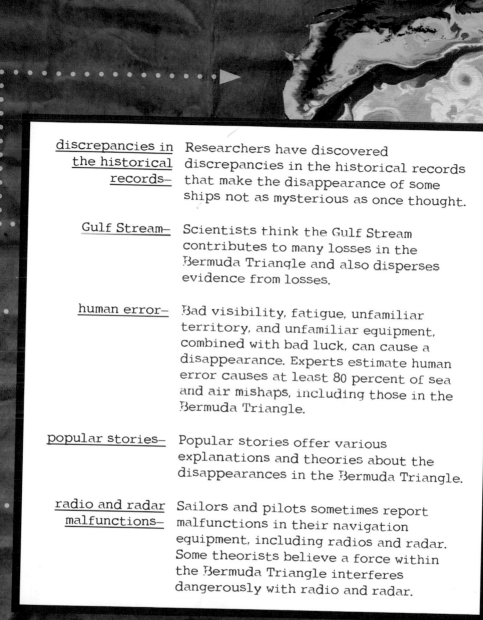

<u>discrepancies in the historical records–</u>	Researchers have discovered discrepancies in the historical records that make the disappearance of some ships not as mysterious as once thought.
<u>Gulf Stream–</u>	Scientists think the Gulf Stream contributes to many losses in the Bermuda Triangle and also disperses evidence from losses.
<u>human error–</u>	Bad visibility, fatigue, unfamiliar territory, and unfamiliar equipment, combined with bad luck, can cause a disappearance. Experts estimate human error causes at least 80 percent of sea and air mishaps, including those in the Bermuda Triangle.
<u>popular stories–</u>	Popular stories offer various explanations and theories about the disappearances in the Bermuda Triangle.
<u>radio and radar malfunctions–</u>	Sailors and pilots sometimes report malfunctions in their navigation equipment, including radios and radar. Some theorists believe a force within the Bermuda Triangle interferes dangerously with radio and radar.

Timeline

<u>9000s BCE</u>	The civilization of Atlantis allegedly flourishes.
<u>1492</u>	Christopher Columbus sees light in the ocean during his expedition from Europe to the Americas.
<u>1840</u>	On August 27, a correspondent in Nassau, Bahamas, writes a letter to the London *Times* about the mystery of an abandoned ship called the *Rosalie*.
<u>1918</u>	The *Cyclops* departs Rio de Janeiro, Brazil, on February 16.

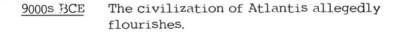

<u>1918</u>	The *Cyclops* stops at Barbados on March 3.
<u>1918</u>	The *Cyclops* leaves Barbados for Chesapeake Bay on March 4 and is never heard from again.

<u>1918</u>	A severe storm batters the North Carolina and Virginia coast on March 9–10, where the *Cyclops* would be if it were still on course.

1918   After a fruitless search, the US Navy
        issues a public statement about the
        loss of the *Cyclops* on April 14.

1925   The *Cotopaxi* departs Charleston,
        South Carolina, for Havana, Cuba, on
        November 29.

1925   All of Florida suffers a severe storm
        on December 1. Florida radio operators
        receive a message from the *Cotopaxi*
        that it is listing badly. It is never
        heard from again.

1941   On November 23, the *Proteus* leaves
        Saint Thomas, Virgin Islands, for
        Portland, Maine.

1941   The *Proteus* is last heard from on
        November 25.

1941   The *Nereus* departs Saint Thomas
        for Portland on December 10.

1941   The *Nereus* is last heard from
        on December 12.

1945   The five planes of Flight 19 perform a
        training exercise between Florida and
        the Bahamas and become lost at sea on
        December 5. A search-and-rescue plane sent
        to find the missing planes explodes.

1945   A huge military and civilian search effort
        from December 5 through December 10 turns
        up no evidence of Flight 19, but does confirm
        the rescue plane's explosion.

Timeline

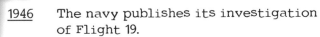

1946 — The navy publishes its investigation of Flight 19.

1947 — After protests from Taylor's family, in October the navy changes its verdict on Flight 19.

1950 — The Associated Press publishes Edward Van Winkle Jones's article "Sea's Puzzles Still Baffle Men In Pushbutton Age" on September 16.

1952 — *Fate* magazine publishes George X. Sand's "Sea Mystery at Our Back Door" in October.

1962 — *American Legion* magazine publishes Allan W. Eckert's "The Mystery of the Lost Patrol" in April.

1962 — Dale Titler publishes, *Wings of Mystery: True Stories of Aviation History*.

1964 — *Argosy* magazine publishes Vincent Gaddis's "The Deadly Bermuda Triangle" in February.

1964	The navy builds its Atlantic Undersea Test and Evaluation Center (AUTEC) in the Bahamas.
1968	A researcher finds an unusual rock formation off the coast of Bimini, Bahamas. Dean Hawes spots a sunken wreck resembling the *Cyclops* near Norfolk, Virginia.
1969	John Spencer publishes *Limbo of the Lost*.
1970	Bruce Gernon allegedly flies through a time-travel cloud in the Bermuda Triangle.
1973	*Naval Aviation News* publishes Michael McDonell's article "Lost Patrol" in June.
1974	Richard Winer publishes *The Devil's Triangle* and releases a documentary film by the same name. Charles Berlitz publishes *The Bermuda Triangle*.
1974	*Sealift* magazine publishes Howard Rosenberg's skeptical article, "Exorcizing the Devil's Triangle," on June 19.
1975	Larry Kusche publishes *The Bermuda Triangle Mystery—Solved*.
1978	A dramatic film based on Berlitz's book hits movie theaters.
1991	Graham Hawkes discovers five Avengers on the seafloor off Fort Lauderdale in May. Inspection reveals the planes are not those used for Flight 19.
2005	Gian J. Quasar publishes *Into the Bermuda Triangle* and Bruce Gernon publishes *The Fog*, causing a modest revival in public interest.

Glossary

aberration . . . . Something that is not normal.

anomaly . . . . Something odd, rare, or out of the ordinary.

dimension . . . . A level of existence or consciousness.

ditch . . . . To make an unplanned sea landing of an airplane.

electromagnetism . . A branch of science that deals with the physical relations between electricity and magnetism.

limbo . . . . A place of uncertainty, unawareness, or neglect.

listing . . . . Tipping or tilting.

paranormal . . . . Outside the range of normal experience or scientific explanation.

propulsion . . . . A force that moves an object forward.

radio frequency . . . . The frequency of motion in the sound waves sent by a radio. A radio frequency is somewhat like a television channel.

skeptic . . . . Someone who tends to doubt or who requires an abundance of evidence before accepting a conclusion.

sonar . . . . A device for detecting and locating objects underwater by the reflection of sound waves.

torpedo bomber . . . . An airplane designed to attack ships by dropping torpedoes, or self-propelling bombs, into the water.

utopian . . . . Ideal.

waterspout . . . . A tornado at sea.

Additional Resources

Selected Bibliography

Burgess, Robert E. *Man: 12,000 Years under the Sea*. Amherst, NY: Dodd, Mead and Company, 1980. Print.

Cotton, John L., and Randall J. Scalise. "The Bermuda Triangle." *The Scientific Method—Critical and Creative Thinking (Debunking Pseudoscience)*. Southern Methodist U, Spring 2011. Web. 27 May 2011.

Gaddis, Vincent H. *Invisible Horizons: True Mysteries of the Sea*. Philadelphia: Chilton, 1965. Print.

Kusche, Larry. *The Bermuda Triangle Mystery—Solved*. Amherst, NY: Prometheus, 1995. Print.

Quasar, Gian J. *Into the Bermuda Triangle: Pursuing the Truth behind the World's Greatest Mystery*. New York: McGraw, 2005. Print.

US Navy. "The Bermuda Triangle." *Naval History and Heritage Command*. n.d. Web. 28 May 2011.

Further Readings

Stewart, Gail B. *The Bermuda Triangle*. San Diego: ReferencePoint, 2009. Print.

Walker, Kathryn. *Mysteries of the Bermuda Triangle*. New York: Crabtree, 2008. Print.

Web Links

To learn more about the Bermuda Triangle, visit ABDO Publishing Company online at **www.abdopublishing.com**. Web sites about the Bermuda Triangle are featured on our Book Links page. These links are routinely monitored and updated to provide the most current information available.

Places to Visit

The Mariners' Museum
100 Museum Drive
Newport News, VA 23606
757-596-2222
http://www.marinersmuseum.org
One of the largest maritime museums in the world, the Mariner's Museum features collections relating to the history of human interaction with the ocean.

National Naval Aviation Museum
1750 Radford Boulevard, Suite C
NAS Pensacola, FL 32508
850-452-3604 or 850-452-3606
http://www.navalaviationmuseum.org
This official Department of the Navy museum preserves and celebrates naval aviation history.

Naval Air Station Fort Lauderdale Museum
4000 West Perimeter Road
Fort Lauderdale, FL 33315
954-359-4400
http://www.nasflmuseum.com
This museum preserves records and artifacts related to the NAS Fort Lauderdale.

Source Notes

Chapter 1. Flight 19

1. Hillary Mayell. "Bermuda Triangle: Behind the Intrigue." *National Geographic News*. National Geographic Society, 15 Dec. 2003. Web. 28 May 2011.

2. Michael McDonell. "Lost Patrol." *Naval Aviation News* (June 1973): 8–16. *Naval History and Heritage Command: Frequently Asked Questions*. Web. 1 June 2011.

3. Ibid.

4. Ibid.

5. Larry Kusche. *The Bermuda Triangle Mystery—Solved*. Amherst, NY: Prometheus, 1995. Print. 105.

6. Ibid. 107.

7. Ibid.

8. Michael McDonell. "Lost Patrol." *Naval Aviation News* (June 1973): 8–16. *Naval History and Heritage Command: Frequently Asked Questions*. Web. 1 June 2011.

9. Larry Kusche. *The Bermuda Triangle Mystery—Solved*. Amherst, NY: Prometheus, 1995. Print. 110.

10. Michael McDonell. "Lost Patrol." *Naval Aviation News* (June 1973): 8–16. *Naval History and Heritage Command: Frequently Asked Questions*. Web. 1 June 2011.

11. Ibid.

12. Harry Allston. "NAS Jacksonville Board of Investigation into 5 Missing TBM Airplanes and One PBM Airplane Convened by Naval Air Advanced Training Command, NAS Jacksonville, Florida 7 December 1945 and Related Correspondence (Flight 19)." *Hyperwar: US Navy in World War II*, n.d. *ibiblio*. Web. 14 June 2011.

13. Ibid.

14. Larry Kusche. *The Bermuda Triangle Mystery—Solved*. Amherst, NY: Prometheus, 1995. Print. 121.

Chapter 2. A Watery Grave

1. Larry Kusche. *The Bermuda Triangle Mystery—Solved*. Amherst, NY: Prometheus, 1995. Print. 24–25.

2. "Collier Overdue a Month." *New York Times*. New York Times, 15 Apr. 1918. Web. 6 June 2011.

3. Alfred P. Reck. "Strangest American Sea Mystery Is Solved At Last." *Popular Science* (June 1929): 15–17, 137. *Google Book Search*. Web. 6 June 2011.

4. Ibid.

5. "Collier Overdue a Month." *New York Times*. New York Times, 15 Apr. 1918. Web. 6 June 2011.

6. Larry Kusche. *The Bermuda Triangle Mystery—Solved*. Amherst, NY: Prometheus, 1995. Print. 76.

Chapter 3. Looking Back on Flight 19

1. E. V. W. Jones. "Sea's Puzzles Still Baffle Men in Pushbutton Age." *Miami Herald*, 17 Sept. 1950: 6F. *Debunking Pseudoscience: Southern Methodist University Physics Department*. Web. 27 May 2011.

2. Ibid.

3. Ibid.

4. Ibid.

5. George X. Sand. "Sea Mystery at Our Back Door." *Fate* (Oct. 1952): 11–17. *Debunking Pseudoscience: Southern Methodist University Physics Department*. Web. 27 May 2011.

6. Ibid.

7. Ibid.

8. Ibid.

9. Ibid.

10. Ibid.

11. Ibid.

Chapter 4. Weaving A Web of Mystery

1. Bill Norrington. "The Geography of the Bermuda Triangle." *UC Santa Barbara Department of Geography Department News*. Regents of the University of California, 1 Sept. 2010. Web. 28 May 2011.

2. Ibid.

3. Vincent H. Gaddis. "The Deadly Bermuda Triangle." *Argosy* (February 1964): 28–29, 116–118. *Debunking Pseudoscience: Southern Methodist University Physics Department*. Web. 27 May 2011.

4. Ibid.

5. Ibid.

6. Ibid.

7. Ibid.

8. Ibid.

9. Ibid.

10. Ibid.

11. "Book [Review]: Richard Winer, 'The Devil's Triangle.'" *Ill-Advised*. Blogspot.com, 23 Feb. 2008. Web. 24 June 2011.

12. Laura Eddie. "The Skeptics SA Guide to the Bermuda Triangle." *Skeptics SA*. Skeptics SA, Jan. 2010. Web. 22 June 2011.

Chapter 5. Blame It on Aliens

1. "Book [Review]: Richard Winer, 'The Devil's Triangle.'" *Ill-Advised*. Blogspot.com, 23 Feb. 2008. Web. 24 June 2011.

2. "Book [Review]: J. W. Spencer, 'Limbo of the Lost—Today'." *Ill-Advised*. Blogspot.com, 10 Nov. 2007. Web. 24 June 2011.

3. Laura Eddie. "The Skeptics SA Guide to the Bermuda Triangle." *Skeptics SA*. Skeptics SA, Jan. 2010. Web. 22 June 2011.

4. Plato. *Timaeus*. Trans. Benjamin Jowett. New York: Scribner's Sons, 1871. *Internet Sacred Text Archive*. Web. 27 June 2011.

5. Ibid.

6. Laura Eddie. "The Skeptics SA Guide to the Bermuda Triangle." *Skeptics SA*. Skeptics SA, Jan. 2010. Web. 22 June 2011.

7. Ibid.

8. Vincent H. Gaddis. "The Deadly Bermuda Triangle." *Argosy* (February 1964): 28–29, 116–118. *Debunking Pseudoscience: Southern Methodist University Physics Department*. Web. 27 May 2011.

9. Ibid.

10. Laura Eddie. "The Skeptics SA Guide to the Bermuda Triangle." *Skeptics SA*. Skeptics SA, Jan. 2010. Web. 22 June 2011.

Chapter 6. Some Facts Are Hard to Ignore

1. Michael McDonell. "Lost Patrol." *Naval Aviation News* (June 1973): 8–16. *Naval History and Heritage Command: Frequently Asked Questions*. Web. 1 June 2011.

2. Ibid.

3. Ibid.

4. Ibid.

5. Ibid.

6. Ibid.

7. Ibid.

8. Ibid.

9. Ibid.

10. Ibid.

11. Howard L. Rosenberg. "Exorcizing the Devil's Triangle." *Sealift* (19 June 1974): 11–15. *Naval History and Heritage Command: Frequently Asked Questions*. Web. 28 May 2011.

12. Ibid.

13. Ibid.

14. Ibid.

15. Ibid.

Chapter 7. <u>A Mystery Solved?</u>

1. Larry Kusche. *The Bermuda Triangle Mystery—Solved*. Amherst, NY: Prometheus, 1995. Print. xiii.

2. Ibid. 77.

3. Ibid. 277.

Chapter 8. <u>The Bermuda Triangle Today</u>

1. Gian J. Quasar. "Skepticism and the Triangle." *Bermuda-Triangle. org*. Bermuda-Triangle.org, 2011. Web. 5 July 2011.

2. Gian J. Quasar. "Bad Navigation?" *Bermuda-Triangle.org*. Bermuda-Triangle.org, n.d. Web. 19 Aug. 2011.

3. "Department of Defense Human Factors Analysis and Classification System: A Mishap Investigation and Data Analysis Tool." *Human Resources: Health, Safety & Work-Life.* United States Coast Guard, n.d. Web. 5 July 2011.

4. "2010 FAASTeam Safety Stand Down." *FAA Safety Team News.* Federal Aviation Administration, May 2010. Web. 5 Jul 2011.

5. Anna Salleh. "Giant Bubbles Could Sink Ships." *Discoverynews. com*. Discovery Communications, 24 Oct. 2003. Web. 30 May 2011.

6. "The Bermuda Triangle." *Naval History and Heritage Command: Frequently Asked Questions*. US Navy, n.d. Web. 28 May 2011.

7. Hillary Mayell. "Bermuda Triangle: Behind the Intrigue." *National Geographic News*. National Geographic Society, 15 Dec. 2003. Web. 28 May 2011.

8. Bill Norrington. "The Geography of the Bermuda Triangle." *UC Santa Barbara Department of Geography Department News*. Regents of the University of California, 1 Sept. 2010. Web. 28 May 2011.

Index

About the Author

Christine Zuchora-Walske has been writing and editing books and magazines for children and their parents for 20 years. Her author credits include natural science titles, books exploring the world's nations, and more. Zuchora-Walske has also edited hundreds of articles and books in many genres and for all ages.

About the Content Consultant

W. Sean Chamberlin teaches oceanography and Earth Science at Fullerton College in Fullerton, California. He has co-authored an oceanography textbook and posted more than 100 ocean-related video lectures on YouTube.

Photo Credits

Lauri Wiberg/iStockphoto, cover, 3, 43; Red Line Editorial, 9, 73; Acey Harper/Time & Life Pictures/Getty Images, 10, 95, 100 (top); Apic/Getty Images, 15, 25, 98, 99 (bottom); Glenn L. Martin Co./AP Images, 18; Kimberly Butler/Time & Life Pictures/ Getty Images, 21; Matt Tilghman/iStockphoto, 23, 105; Bain News Service/Library of Congress, 29, 99 (top); AP Images, 33, 64, 84, 89, 96 (bottom), 100 (bottom), 101; Mary Evans Picture Library/ Alamy, 37, 61; Emory Kristof/National Geographic/Getty Images, 40; Buyenlarge/Getty Images, 46; Sunn Classic Pictures/Photofest, 51; Library of Congress, 53; DEA PICTURE LIBRARY/De Agostini/Getty Images, 55; Stephen Frink Collection/Alamy, 56; Steve Mann/Shutterstock Images, 67, 97 (bottom); Steve Nicklas, NOS, NGS/National Oceanic and Atmospheric Administration, 71; Hulton Archive/Getty Images, 77; Shutterstock Images, 81; Bob Evans, Peter Minnett, & co-workers/University of Miami/ Visible Earth/NASA, 87, 97 (top); Gary McIntyre/Bigstock, 90, 96 (top)